D1622100

Finding Freedom

Also by Bruce Bruinsma

Moving Forward and

The Retirement Reformation

FINDING FREEDOM

Understanding The Power Of A Future Funded Ministry

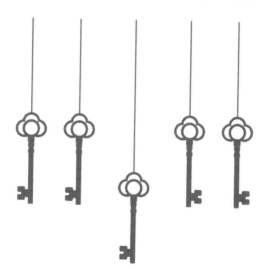

BRUCE BRUINSMA

Print Edition

Published by Envoy Financial

CONTENTS

INTRODUCTION

In the Beginning

In the mid-80s, the results of the Baby Boomer generation growth was starting to show. Christian ministries realized that member care, as it's called in Mission Organizations, is important to keeping staff for the long term. Ministry workers were vaguely aware of the need to prepare for a longer lifespan and did not know how to do it. The financial side of the long-term preparation was pretty much a dark hole.

In the late 80s, and still today, workers in vocational ministry needed help with investing and retirement planning. My call to ministry emerged. It was to respond to the mounting need that missionaries and ministers needed serious retirement planning help. Three decades later, the need still exists. It was clear to me then and now that Christians are all called to a lifetime of ministry but are not preparing for it. With the proper planning, a lifetime of ministry leads inevitably to ministry for a lifetime.

What does it mean to be called to a lifetime of ministry?

Well, there is a common duty (or call) to all Christians to be ministers, impact others, and help change lives. This primary call is to have a personal relationship with Jesus. Now you have a changed life—yours! Remember when those changes started? The relief, the weight lifted off your shoulders? You were so happy that you wanted to tell others and to help others too.

In addition to this primary call extended to all, there is also an individual call to serve—a uniquely personal call extended by God to each and every Jesus follower. This secondary call is an exciting one too. How you are called and uniquely prepared to serve is entirely different from everyone else. Like snowflakes, no two are the same. Yours will be different from how your pastor, your friends, your coworkers, your children, or how anyone else will serve. You are created special and unique in God's eyes.

The Bible speaks to all of us, not only to those in full-time ministry and leadership but also to all of us who fill the pews each Sunday:

"Shepherd the flock of God that is among you, exercising oversight, not under compulsion, but willingly, as God would have you; not for shameful gain, but eagerly; not domineering over those in your charge, but being examples to the flock."
1 Peter 5:2-3

The Time Has Come

My goal is to help you to understand your call, recognize the preparation needed, and know how to respond. What does it mean to be faithful for a lifetime? When believers understand the need to plan and prepare for the time when the paycheck stops, the opportunities to serve expands exponentially.

Serving for a lifetime and helping to support those in need and those who have not yet heard the message then goes from theory to practice. It is important to start preparing for a lifetime of ministry now, which will extend to the very end of your life. In other words, we need to understand, prepare, and fund our future. Flexibility with our time and expanded choice because of sufficient resources are levers that open doors to ministry for a lifetime. It is critical to put dollars away now for all the additional years of ministry ahead—your Future Funded Ministry.

Key Themes

When you embrace the idea of Future Funded Ministry by embarking on this meaningful journey, there are a few fundamental themes and perspectives to explore. These themes will imprint Future Funded Ministry on your mind and heart.

Therefore, our first steps on the journey will:

- Debunk the myth surrounding retirement

- Realize that we are living longer than ever

- Understand our Christian commitment to represent Jesus

- Discover Future Funded Ministry in depth

- Embrace Future Funded Ministry as critical to your life's mission

A Journey of Discovery and Hope

This book is indeed a journey of discovery and hope. I will help you find out for yourself what Future Funded Ministry can mean to you and others. To do this, I've separated this book into four clear sections.

In the **first section**, I clearly define what it means to retire. Then, we will look at how Future Funded Ministry is uniquely designed to give you the power necessary for a meaningful, rich, and God-honoring retirement.

In the **second section**, I demonstrate through the failures of real people how poor planning, mismanagement of finances, and the happenstance of life can adversely impact the lives of all that do not plan and prepare for meaningful ministry in their golden years.

I have dedicated the **third section** to life examples of those who understand the power of Future Funded Ministry. These "champions" stand firmly behind the ideas of Future Funded Ministry, and they are excited to share their stories with you. They want you to see through their eyes and lives what the power of Future Funded Ministry can do for you.

The **final section** helps tie it all together and shares our expanded concept of the DNA of meaning: a lifetime of purpose. How you can live a truly meaningful life—a life full of purpose and the joy that comes with it—a life energized by the power of Future Funded Ministry.

What This Book is Not

This book is not about saving, investing, or budgeting, although these are important topics. This book will not tell you how to prepare, but it is a book about preparation. This book will not make you an investment guru or anything close, but it will provide the encouragement and insights to learn and do more. This book is about the "why" that leads to the "how."

The next book in this series, Moving Forward: Putting your Future Funded Ministry in Motion, deals with the "how" questions. You will understand Future Funded Ministry and how to move forward when you engage with its content.

Now Let's Begin

Retirement is not only a reward for past service,
it is a stepping stone to future ministry.

Bruce Bruinsma

To understand this better, let's start at the point of retirement. Let's start with the end in mind, and explore it from our western, cultural perspective. The goal of this next section is to help you forget everything you thought you knew about retirement and to think about it in a whole new way—a more meaningful and compelling way and an approach that will transform your life!

1

The Retirement Dream Myth

Retirement is the dream of many. Men often say, "When I retire, I will have my own designated seat at the 19th hole, and every morning my buddies will meet me for breakfast, and we'll decide whether to play eighteen or drop a line in the water. I'll never miss another big game on my large screen TV, and my wife and I will grow old together, happily, and comfortably until the end of our days." The vision is clear and the stress reduction compelling.

Retirement is the dream of many women who often say, "I'm going to get myself a cozy little place by the beach and watch the sun disappear into the ocean. I will jog along the shoreline and sip a Mai Tai every night. My husband will sit beside me in his lounger while our dog frolics in the waves. I'll have multiple cups of coffee or tea or maybe some fruit juice with my new friends. We can play tennis until the courts close. The grandchildren will be both loving and available." The vision is clear and the stress reduction compelling.

Perhaps these words, or ones with similar meaning, reflect your dreams of retirement? Maybe you connect this message with the retirement ads on TV, in newspapers, or in magazines? Perhaps you dream of retiring and moving to warmer or more beautiful climates—a move to Florida, Arizona, or California. Or, at the other extreme, do you think that you will never slow down? For many, the dreams bring some confusion about priorities and result in ducking the issues entirely.

Change Your Life. Change the World.

As one minister said, "I'll just die in the pulpit." Perhaps some entertain the fantasy of moving to the mountains to hike, ski, kayak inlets, or find hidden gems of lakes to fish; to go places that have communities of people just like yourselves; or to head off far away to the tropics where you can go live the rest of your days in quiet solitude. For others, there is the belief that they will work until the day they die. And even as they get closer to that time and their body slows down, they can't imagine a day when they aren't working, and frankly, don't want to imagine one. We have all come face to face with this myth of retirement stated in a thousand different, yet similar, ways. And then there are some, even many, that don't dream about it at all. The financial realities of life don't allow them to even entertain a future different from their past. If we don't change, the future will look very much like the past.

Jesus said, "I have come to change the world..."

You are a part of that world.

Dreams. Dreams. Dreams.

These fantastic interludes of the mind, these forays into what, as young people, middle-aged, and even senior citizens think retirement should be, are all just that—forays into fantasy. Around age fifty, things start to change and fears about our physical, mental, and financial reality set in. While we recognize that the truth will set us free, we seldom venture very far into a new and vital future. You don't know you are stuck until you try to pull yourself out of the mud.

Not only do adults in midlife realize that these dreamy visions of glorious retirement are the thoughts of those too young to appreciate the actual number of years still ahead, but they also gain a new understanding of how long retirement can be. Along with the appreciation of an extended time horizon comes the realization about the potential those years can hold. There is an excellent potential and significant meaning ahead. Life is filled with fruitful activity, both satisfying to you and positively impacting others.

Is There Purpose?

Expected questions arise: is there a purpose and a greater meaning for my life beyond these fantasies? What will I still be able to do? How can I realistically plan? Is it too late? How will I continue to find meaning in my daily existence? Can I get on track? Does God still have a purpose for me to fulfill? Do I understand what it is?

Now is the time for a new understanding to emerge—that there really is more. Life still has a purpose. God prepares us to minister for a lifetime, not just a season. New insights explode, and a powerful new understanding and a new vision emerge. We realize the power inherent in the idea of Future Funded Ministry. You can be excited about the future. I am—come join me.

The next big question then is how will we (and can we) fund our future ministry? Yes, there is an important money component. We ask, "Will we be financially ready as well as physically, emotionally, and spiritually prepared to step into our future?"

Face it: For the majority of people, "Florida or Arizona" is not a viable option. And you know what they say about "too much of a good thing" anyway. For just a few moments, think about what it might be like to play golf every day or fish or travel all the time. Sound good? Some days it does. However, because it has little meaning and no eternal purpose, it will get old, stale, and even boring. Your hobby becomes your work, and the par 3 replaces your Tuesday morning metrics review. You no longer appreciate the joys of your favorite hobbies or pastime activities. Hobbies were pleasurable distractions from everyday life—they represented the things you craved during your pre-retirement years. You could not get enough of them. Your priorities of living got in the way. Work, your family, and those dutiful responsibilities took all of your time. The escapes from work become the dreams of retirement. We dream about doing those things full time during retirement. Unfortunately, it becomes a reality without a purpose—a dream without meaning. Fishing an errant golf ball from the water hazard does not bring the same sense of fulfillment as helping a boy without a dad grow into a man with a purpose.

Do Nothing

Let me insert a word about "nothing." Nothing is a frequent response to the question, "What are you going to do when you retire?" This answer suggests either no interests, no understanding of God's ongoing call on your life, or the result of intentionally postponing all plans for your future. Unfortunately, nothing is becoming an all too typical response. I've started reacting to the "nothing" response with this question, "I wonder how long it takes to become tired of nothing?"

Truly the balance of the meaningful and pleasurable is what provides the spice of life. That balance here on earth is valuable. It is valuable to live every day striving to understand God's plan for us for today. Now is an excellent time to reflect on the catechism answer to the question: What is the chief end of man? The answer: Man's chief end is to glorify God and enjoy Him forever. We are called to a relationship with God first. Then as a reflection of our gratitude for His grace and our eternal salvation, we respond by looking outward in service. Both our vertical and horizontal relationships are valuable. Out of the being (who we are) comes the doing (what we do).

Meaning with true purpose is one of life's important values. My desire is for you to be motivated to live out those values for a lifetime. Fulfilling God's plan for your life does bring balance, joy, accomplishment, and meaning. That combination then leads to a full, complete existence. Faithful for a lifetime goes from being a nice thought to a meaningful reality.

As you get closer to retirement, you realize that you want to be faithful to His plan and purpose. There is not only value created but personal equity too. You are creating value that lasts for a lifetime.

Empty nests are good homes for expanding inspired ministry. Your pre-retirement life was goal-oriented. Hard work was the hallmark of your days. The result of hard work is goals accomplished and mission completed. You achieved and succeeded in multiple ways, experiencing highs and lows and often highs again. You now realize a focus on pleasurable hobbies and other sometimes fun but non-productive distractions are not enough.

A meaningful senior life with its different life stages calls for more, much more. As you approach 65 or 67 or 68, it's imperative not to stop but to continue with meaningful activities. Those activities will further the Kingdom and bring deep personal satisfaction. When those activities reflect God's plan, times are good. And yes, there will still be time for golf.

Transforming unreal dreams into a lifetime of purpose is not a myth, but it is God's call being played out in each of our lives—the call being played out with power, purpose, and Kingdom impact.

2

We Are Living Longer Than Ever

It's a fact that people are living longer than ever before. According to the U.S. Census Bureau, since 1970 there is about an eight-year increase in longevity. The eight-year increase in lifespan is true for both genders. Most people live well into their 80s, and there are more centenarians and super-centenarians alive than ever before.

According to the National Institute on Aging (NIH), life expectancy nearly doubled during the 20th century with a tenfold increase in the number of Americans age 65 or older. There are approximately 35 million Americans age 65 or older, and we will see it double to 70 million in the next 25 years. The oldest old—people age 85 or older—constitute the fastest growing segment of the U.S. population—about four million people. This population will top 19 million by 2050 as living to 100 becomes increasingly commonplace. In 1950 there were approximately 3,000 American centenarians, by 2050 there will be nearly one million. Yes, a million more really old people. The odds are good that you will be amongst them or you will know many who are.

Reflecting on the realities of today, many Baby Boomers are well into retirement now. This largest and longest living generation of Americans is going to exist without paychecks (or at a reduced paycheck) for many, many years. We have an obvious problem. You do know the paycheck will stop, don't you? The next question is, what do we do?

Today, when people "retire" they often remain in the workforce. They go part-time or find part-time jobs. They become "you name it" emeritus or become an advisor or infrequent consultant. There are two reasons for this. They need ancillary income or they simply, as we have already said, need meaningful ways to occupy their new flex time status. You need meaning to experience a fulfilled life.

Strange as it sounds, dreading retirement is increasingly true for many in the pre-55 crowd. They dread the word, ignore the realities, and don't prepare for the inevitable. You may even hear yourself say things like, "I will never retire." The idea of retirement is nothing to fear when you've prepared. It's something to think about in new God-honoring ways. With a new mindset, the next step is to listen carefully and plan wisely.

Digging Deeper

The next few chapters are devoted to a redefinition and deeper understanding of retirement. This redefined retirement includes the marvelous new perspective I call Future Funded Ministry. I expect you will begin to understand how these tenets align with your life's purpose and with God's divine plan. Then and only then will fear dissipate. You will embrace a new way of thinking and appreciate the empowered freedom and new energy now embodied in your Future Funded Ministry.

Please understand that as you grow older, your body will prompt you to slow down. Within reason, it's important that you listen and begin operating at a somewhat slower pace but with a similar intensity and motivated purpose. It's time you think about and plan for the next stages of life with purpose as you get closer to retirement. You can do this—you can connect both a meaningful life and a fun life with purpose if you embrace it right now and put a plan in place to fund it.

Preparation is Important

I've asked you to give up the frivolous, retain the fun, and focus on God's plan for the rest of your life. So, what gives life meaning? Not in the general sense but specifically for you? What current activities reflect your life priorities? How has God prepared you for the next stage of your life, and then the next? Reading, praying, and reflecting on Psalm 32 is an excellent place to start. Pay close attention to the verses:

You are my hiding place,
You will preserve me from trouble,
You will surround me with songs of deliverance.

I will instruct you and teach you on the way you should go.

I will counsel you and watch over you!

But he who trusts in the Lord, mercy shall surround him.

And then, rejoice in the Lord and be glad.

The whole Psalm, especially those words, give instruction, comfort, and encouragement. You will connect with God's plan for you. You will recognize how He's prepared you. And how He gives you the strength to embrace His chosen path for you.

3

We Are All Ministers Together

There is another side to all of this that is equally important. As Christians, we believe we are challenged to use our unique gifts to give, teach, support, and love for a lifetime. This is our crucible—the place where meaning and action intersect and reveal part of God's divine plan. Ministry is the grace-filled outcome of this intersection and the changes made in people's lives.

Ministry is a call on our lives. A joyful response posing as a duty that we pledge and practice love, giving, and compassion—through our hands, our heads, and our hearts—to our neighbors and those less fortunate than ourselves. We are challenged to help many to grow as Christians, so they too can help change the lives of others. We are all ministers together, life changers, and therefore challenged to give back during all of our years.

It is important that we consider some basic tenets of ministry and what constitutes a call to ministry. Remember, every one of us who follows Jesus is a minister and has a call.

What is ministry? An easy yet insightful way to think about it is: ministry is changing lives. Yes, if you think about it, it's indeed that simple. And because we are dealing with people, it is also complicated. We have both a common call to ministry reflected in our overall responsibility as Christians, and then each of us has a personal call to ministry. Our common or primary call starts with a relationship with God. We are called primarily to Him, and then with gratitude, we accept our secondary call.

This call is a personal one. One that God determines and only we can define, express, and act upon. Our ministry is at once extrinsic and intrinsic, or maybe it's better to say that there are societal rewards, inner fulfillment, and eternal values as part of it.

Ministers come in all shapes and sizes. Most of us may think first of pastors, preachers, and priests, or maybe the lay ministers that help guide us with Sunday service. But the reality is that ministry is the calling of every Christian—every human being really—who believes that meaning is derived from our spiritual relationships, rewarding work, the love of our families, and serving the people around us. Ministry means changing lives and providing for those who cannot provide for themselves, and it means making it possible for others to do these great acts of love and kindness. We either act directly, or we facilitate the actions of others. Both are valuable. We are to reflect Jesus to our world, and we are each uniquely equipped for that service.

Your Call to Ministry

So what then constitutes your call to ministry? I believe there are four elements to produce a valid and obedient call (that counsel of God mentioned in Psalms):

1. The first element is a strong personal conviction or motivation felt by an individual to engage in

something very specific that enters and impacts the lives of others. This activity is not a one-time occurrence, but it's likely that we will have multiple calls during our life.

2. The second element is identified as "effective enablement." Effective enablement can come through general life experiences, education, or very specific personal events and occurrences. In some cases, the enablement is developed during a relatively brief period, while in others, it may take decades. It can involve such things as skills (like healing arts and speaking), knowledge (such as foreign languages and biblical knowledge), attitudes (like mercy and courage), and personality traits (such as gentleness and boldness).

3. The third element is opportunity. We have the opportunity to carry out the ministry to which we are called. An opportunity can be spontaneous and short-lived, occurring as an encounter on the street, in a store, or in a tragic emergency. It can also be long-term, to the point that a particular life path opens up one situation after another to impact individuals in one-on-one encounters or with large groups. God knows when and where our motiva-

tion, enablement, and opportunity come together. When there is convergence, we are put in the right place at the right time to serve others' needs and to do the right thing. It is the Holy Spirit that whispers in our ear to "go and do."

4. The last element is that we are to surrender to God's leadership and to each specific prompting He delivers. Specifically, it does no good to have motivation, enablement, and opportunity if we don't step up and do what's needed right then, when, and where it's needed. The surrender might be just a few moments, an interruption to our day to address a person in need. Or it can be a long time—maybe, even an entire lifetime—the willingness to be devoted to a singular cause or type of ministry.

It Started in Timbuktu

My calling to Timbuktu is a good example of God's prompting, my response, and a key lesson learned. The lesson? When God calls, I will go. It was and is important to understand what obedience looks like. What lessons have you learned? Perhaps, what lessons are still to come? Growing in our relationship with

God and practicing listening to His voice is a never-ending curriculum of life.

We've established that our pre-retirement lives are full of highs and lows, rewards and pain, meaning and despair. Hopefully, we learn something from all of these experiences. I try to examine each experience for the message, lesson learned, or new direction discovered. Maybe there is something that is awakening in you now—something that was always there but never acknowledged. A gentle whisper in your ear or a tug on your heart. A quiet moment of reflection along with an open Bible often brings amazing insights. I often turn to the books of wisdom and life experiences such as the Psalms or Proverbs. Initially, I was surprised at how God spoke to my issue in those words. Today I'm expectant—not surprised.

A Call to ACTION

Our call to ministry is demonstrated by our actions. Our actions do speak louder than our words or even our thoughts. We serve our Lord as servant leaders for our employer and employees. We are dutiful to our families, and we derive joy from the things we accomplish, the money we earn, and our ability to protect, treasure, raise, and nurture our loved ones. We also find and embrace acts of kindness, and in giving, we see a higher purpose. We engage every day understanding our mission of reflecting Jesus to the world. God puts us here to support charitable causes and help those less fortunate than ourselves.

This meaningfulness, this purpose to our life-changing reflected ministry, is what brings value to our very existence. So when the paycheck stops, the kids are grown, and it's just you and your spouse living out your days, this is when new or additional ministry can flourish. While ministry flourishes, you need to get out and play a little golf or travel to Paris or Israel or Suriname. It's in this balance between ministry and new experiences that we thrive. Here is where we find the emotional energy to answer the call and to serve as ministers together.

To truly engage your call for a lifetime, you need a plan. Being willing to go, serve, love, and support is foundational, but it is not enough. It's imperative to prepare, and a critical element in that preparation is funding your future ministry. To effectively go about funding your future, it is best to start as early as you can. At some level we all know this is true—it is just that so many do not do it. Start now because a future without funding is a life without focus. Or, all the focus will be on the lack of money in the future. God's word says "prepare."

4

Re-Thinking Retirement

The meaning of Retirement needs significant rethinking. Let's start with this thought: the future must be funded, and ministry must continue or new ministries begun after retirement. So, let's start to redefine it. From now on, let's refer to this state of financial preparedness for retirement officially as "Future Funded Ministry." In my book entitled, The Retirement Reformation, I expand on the meaning of retirement beyond the financial component. While a holistic view of retirement is important, putting your Future Funded Ministry into motion is critical.

Realize there is a dream, maybe not one from your youth, but the one that includes a meaningful life of value and impact. A life you can continue—one that has a true balance between what you give back to the world and what the world gives back to you. You have your common and personal ministry to accomplish through the last three stages of your life, ages: 67-77, 77-87, and 87 on.

Part of our understanding of retirement, including the Future Funded Ministry part, is realizing that there are three different life stages before retirement and three life stages during retirement.

Pre-Retirement life stages:

Just starting out: 20 to 39
Picking up speed: 40 to 54
Almost there 55+

Three stages during retirement:

Active Application: 67 to 78
(early retirement)

Insightful Stewardship: 69 to 87
(middle retirement)

Reflective Sharing: 88+
(late retirement)

Early retirement: The ability and capacity to put into practice what you have learned up to this point in your life. You can lead, be very productive, and bring energy to all your endeavors.

Middle retirement: The ability to bring wisdom and insight to any opportunity or situation through mentoring. Leadership roles will be collaborative and marked by the ability to bring perspective, support, and encouragement to those who will lead in the future. You will bring value to any discussion or decision.

Late Retirement: The ability to reflect on life's experiences and provide wisdom in helpful and insightful ways for subsequent generations increases. The benefits of longevity will be clear. The contribution to their well-being and Kingdom building skills will be significant. As health deteriorates, wisdom accelerates.

When we understand and model the characteristics of each life stage, we impact those coming behind, provide a road map for ongoing success, enhance our own lives, and provide ongoing energy to build the Kingdom.

Retirement Goals

Here are a few general retirement goals:

- Continue to serve the Lord faithfully and grow spiritually

- Seamlessly support your family

- Do more of the things you have always wanted to do

- Live comfortably and happily with both love and compassion

- Live a life filled with meaning created by your acts of ministry and time spent with others, your community, and your church

Future Funded Ministry gives you the capacity to serve where and when called:

- It's devoted to the devoted—we are all ministers.

• It provides a way to help yourself serve God as a minister.

• It enables missionaries, church employees, and the staff of Christian organizations to plan and wisely manage money for their futures during their income-producing years. And the rest of us too.

• It puts the focus on God's plan, not our own.

• It empowers you to act now. It will help you learn about your Money Personalities and how to deal with money, to accept that you will retire—although with a new definition—and to start to fund it now and embrace its meaning and give flexibility in the future.

There is a parable in the Bible that talks about remaking or reshaping "marred" or flawed materials into something new and useful; it is not unlike the idea that you can reshape your retirement perspective.

5

Making Critical Decisions

The Potter and the Clay

The word which came to Jeremiah from the Lord, saying: "Arise and go down to the potter's house, and there I will cause you to hear My words." Then I went down to the potter's house, and there he was, making something at the wheel. And the vessel that he made of clay was marred in the hand of the potter; so he made it again into another vessel, as it seemed good to the potter to make.

Then the word of the Lord came to me, saying: "O house of Israel, can I not do with you as this potter?" says the Lord. "Look, as the clay is in the potter's hand, so are you in My hand, O house of Israel!

Jeremiah 18:1-6, New King James Version (NKJV)

It's time we re-molded the clay that shapes our perceptions of the time in our lives when the paycheck stops. Let's redefine retirement as something that serves our yearning for both meaning and changed lives; let's embrace the idea of Future Funded Ministry. It brings choice, flexibility, and new power to our lives.

Future Funded Ministry will help you realize your dream and fulfill God's specific plan for you; because face it, dreams need to be planned and funded with real dollars. And dreams aren't just those youthful fantasies—you can discover ways to deliver meaning with impact along with all the good times to come. And then there is the issue of funding—you must fund your future ministry. To help you live it, say it now:

Retirement is not only a reward for past service but a stepping stone for future ministry.

How God Provides

What happens if you don't fund your future? It's worth asking what life will look like if you don't. If you hadn't discovered Future Funded Ministry, how would your life look?

> *Like clouds and wind with rain*
> *Is a man who boasts of gifts*
> *He does not give*
> Psalms 25:14

What follows is my perspective gained from 30 years of helping Christians plan for their future. Not everyone prepares for "golden years." These words emerge from too many planning meetings:

"God will provide."

Yes, that is true: God does provide, and He affords each of us the opportunity to make critical decisions, ones that impact our future. Ones that determine life's path—our unique journey with and for Him. While God owns it all, He charges us with the responsibility to oversee how His resources are used. Money, indeed, does not grow on trees and it is not mystically available for the devout. We are all provided unique opportunities and critical decisions to make. We have responsibilities to ourselves, our family, and to God. Of course, we have all heard of the "money showing up" miracles. At rare times money and other resources do come from surprising places: inheritance, donations, and sometimes even stranger ones. Planning, however, is God's directed way to prepare for your future and the Bible echoes that notion.

We hear about this truth literally and figuratively in Luke 14:28-30:

"For which of you, desiring to build a tower, does not first sit down and count the cost, whether he has enough to complete it? Otherwise, when he has laid a foundation and is not able to finish, all who see it begin to mock him, saying, 'This man began to build and was not able to finish.'"

Finish What We Start by Being Faithful

We must finish what God prompts us to start. And how do we do that? We pray, we plan, we spend/invest accordingly, and we fund our ministry for the future.

In this next section of the book, we explore what pain comes to good people—real people we know. All of the following stories are real, and every one of them explores the failures caused by poor planning, mismanaged expectations, or the wish to do more than is financially possible. Jesus multiplied loaves and fishes in an instant; it takes longer for us.

The Story of John & Mary Plus Bob & Shirley

John, with his bride Mary's help, founded a church, raised a family, and faithfully served a congregation of 125 people. These two grew up together, and they indeed grew old together. The church board changed over the years, as boards do, but honestly not very much. For the most part, the board was highly supportive of John and his ideas. They even built the additional two classrooms on the church for an expanded Sunday School at his request. Whenever the piano needed tuning, they approved the expenditure without fail. But never once did the board mention anything thing about caring for John and Mary's future. They did not discuss the future direction of the church when John left, retired, or died.

A few years ago, the board, with John's blessing, hired

a young man right out of Bible School to be the youth pastor. It was a part-time position, and the young Pastor Bob and his wife both had to work other part-time jobs to make ends meet. The expectation for Bob (and his wife Shirley) was that John and Mary would have to retire soon and he presumed that if he did a good job, the board would move Bob up into the senior pastor position.

John turned 70. But there was a foundational problem—one neither John nor Bob thought or knew about—and the board had not identified. The reality was that John couldn't afford to retire. There was no retirement plan in place—no Future Funded Ministry. His retirement income was his church salary, and there was no backup plan. If the church no longer paid John, then John and Mary's income would drop to zero. John, Mary, the Board, plus Bob and Shirley had a big problem. And there would be no apparent answer to the problem. John couldn't retire and hasn't. Bob could not move up. The church, unfortunately, was shrinking as well, and the alternatives provide only unanswerable headaches.

So what happened? Bob and Shirley left to start a new church. This church began to decline—along with

John and Mary. It was a quiet, but tragic ending to one of God's mission outposts because John's ministry did not recognize the need for a Future Funded Ministry plan.

We Can Plan

It is disheartening to see that all of us, even those with the best intentions and warmest hearts, struggle to make wise choices throughout our lives. And it's true—many outcomes are beyond our control. We do, however, have the ability to plan for our retirement. We can start today to fund our future ministries; we can seize control of the golden years and perhaps even do our best, most meaningful work in those years if we start to steward the dollars away now and invest them wisely.

Some facts cannot be avoided:

1. You will grow older and most likely cease to earn a regular paycheck.

2. If you don't plan for your retirement years, your actions will be unfocused, random, and only lived out in response to the challenge of the moment.

Fulfilling a lifetime of ministry with meaning and purpose will be an illusion.

Growing older doesn't mean that you stop following your heart and your vision for the future—the vision God has already implanted deep within you. And if you plan for retirement by funding your future ministry, you will fulfill the desires of your heart all the way to the very end.

...

What follows are first-hand accounts of what it means to champion your Future Funded Ministry. Meet those who connected with Future Funded Ministry and decided to respond. Meet the true believers, read the impactful stories, and hear what committed champions have to say.

Over the next few pages, you'll meet some very different people with very different life experiences. Yet all of them have a strong Christian belief system and a very powerful respect for Future Funded Ministry. These Future Funded Ministry champion stories are here to inspire you as you begin to apply it to yourself, your church, or your Christian organization. All of these champions understand that our call to ministry is extremely personal and a mandate for all our days. Each firmly believes changing lives and inspiring others is who they are and what they called to do. Now, read a little about them, what makes them tick, and how they believe Future Funded Ministry changes everything.

6

A Future Funded Ministry Champion

Paul Miller is Professor Emeritus Accounting at UCCS—Academic Advisor PGA Golf Management Program and one of America's Top 100 Most Influential People by Accounting Today magazine. Miller is recognized for his advocacy of accounting standards and encouragement of debate about the adoption of International Financial Reporting Standards.

For Paul, his pivotal moment came during a summer break from college, at a regular summer job. He traveled far from his college in Texas to the Rocky Mountains of Colorado to work a busboy job at the YMCA in Estes Park. While Paul was not particularly religious, it was there in the mountains—God's country—that he found his calling in life. During a walk in the woods by himself, he had his first real conversation with God. God spoke to him among the beauty of nature, explaining that all surrounding him was His creation, Paul too was His creation, and that Paul had a responsibility to serve.

In that single moment, surrounded by absolute beauty, Paul understood that the rest of his life would be devoted to God and the love of Christ. He found his calling to serve. Everything fell into place and became crystal clear.

It was in this place, not too long after that walk in the woods, that Paul met the love of his life and she has been his wife for more than 45 years. Even at that age, they were both willing to give of themselves to help others. He recalls their first moments together were spent doing work no one else was willing to do. Ministry brought them together and kept them together. Together, they have spent a lifetime ministering through different channels.

It's possible that Paul's life from the very start was a miracle. Paul was the last of 8 children. His mother, a woman struggling with cancer, managed to give birth to him on a day of peace, the day that World War

II ended. Paul sees all these things, things that other people may call coincidences, as a sign that he was meant for a greater purpose in life—to be a minister. The start of his life, just as the rest of it, was a gift from God and he's spent it helping others.

Paul and his wife have three children, all of whom Paul considers miracles—two sons and a daughter. All are healthy and happy and ministering in their own ways. Both of Paul's sons are pastors at their respective churches, a fact that blesses Paul immensely. They both initially made careers outside the church but were powerfully drawn to minister and serve God. He adopted his daughter from Russia, "brought to them by God," in his words. Paul's daughter made it her life's goal to make sure no children are hurt as she was. As a social worker, she continually impacts the lives of children who have no one else to care for them. Paul knows she's ministering in her own way—protecting children and making sure they have families and homes, just like Paul and his wife provided for her.

Paul's children and their families, just like Paul and his wife, felt the call of God. Paul takes complete pride in the fact that both his sons are pastors with large congregations, and his daughter has her own unique way to minister. Paul's children also understand another facet of Paul—he's an investor in the future.

If there is anything he feels that he has ingrained in his children, it's these two fundamental ways to live:

- Give back, help people, and find your ministry.

- Prepare for your future by smart savings and investments.

Paul explained to them the idea of Future Funded Ministry. They have to have the resources and the ability to continue in order to do their work. Paul wants more than anything else to see his family continue their work as ministers—no matter what age they reach.

In front of his eyes, he saw Future Funded Ministry propel his family's future dreams, both for him and his wife and his children. Paul understands the importance of continuing ministry, no matter his age, and has helped his children understand this too. He knows there is no shame—it is not a lack of faith, and moreover, it is the right thing for a Christian to do— to have a retirement plan, a Future Funded Ministry, to make sure the good work they do will continue until the end of their days.

Faith in Action

Paul told us a parable of his own on this point. He told us of a man who had an unbreakable faith in the Lord:

One day it started flooding near this man's home, and he heard a warning on TV to evacuate. His wife asked him, "What should we do?" And he said, "God will provide." It kept raining hard, and a policeman came by and knocked on his door. The policeman said, "The rain is going to make it flood here. You need to leave." His wife asked him, "What should we do?" And he said, "God will provide." It started to flood, and water flowed into their house. The Coast Guard came by in a boat and said, "Sir, we need to evacuate!" His wife asked him, "What should we do?" and he said, "God will provide." Eventually, his house flooded and a helicopter came for them. "Get in the basket, and we'll take you to safety," said the helicopter pilot. His wife asked him, "What should we do?" And he said, "God will provide." The man and his wife eventually drowned. They arrived in heaven, and the man was angry. He looked up at God said, "Why didn't you provide when I needed you most?" And God said, " I did provide. I provided you a warning on TV, the police, the Coast Guard, and even a helicopter."

The lesson to take from this story is one that Paul lives by. He will tell you about the importance of making the right decisions. The importance of building a financial pathway allowing him to continue responding to God's call. So he in his way and his children in theirs can be faithful for a lifetime. God provides by giving us a role and a pathway. We are good stewards when we follow the star he created for us.

Christian stewardship is God's provision. By being a good steward, Paul takes responsibility for his actions and responsibility for his life. The guiding light among all of this is God. He leads the way; we follow.

Today, Paul teaches Sunday school to seniors while his wife teaches preschoolers. Between the two of them, they cover generations of believers. They minister to them and help them understand the value of ministry and the importance of being a life-changing agent.

Paul is now retired, and though he sometimes moonlights as Professor Emeritus of Accounting at UCCS, he knows and accepts that his body is slowing down. His will and commitment to the principles of Future Funded Ministry have not. He has impacted many and ministered in a multitude of ways. Because he believes so firmly in the principles of Future Funded Ministry, he began preparing long ago for his life today. He can still give back and continue his ministry while supporting organizations and missionaries who in turn give back. His future is now, and he lives his Future Funded Ministry with joy.

7

Walking in Faith & Preparing for Action

Dan is a retired Professor of Anthropology and Translation and Senior Anthropology Consultant for Fuller's Graduate School of Intercultural Studies. He is also a Certified Senior Anthropology Consultant at SIL International. In 1969 he first visited Papua New Guinea as both an anthropologist and a missionary bringing the Bible and its translation to the Samo tribe.

For Dan Shaw, it was obvious he was going to follow in his family's footsteps. There was never any question in his mind about what his earthly purpose would be. Born in India, he always dreamed that he would return to that beautiful country and continue the work that his father (and grandfather before) did. They were missionaries, and his dream was to be a missionary spreading God's word in India and throughout the world. An unexpected curve in the road led him down the path that he would eventually follow.

Around the time that Dan was ready to graduate from College, the Indian government put restrictions on the passage of missionaries to India. United States citizens could no longer get missionary visas into India. The disappointment of not being able to continue the work of his family was devastating. The dream of going to India was over but not the goal of making a difference. The only question was where–not if he was to go.

Dan was finishing a master's degree in Anthropology at the University of Arizona. Being so close to graduation, with only three credits left to complete, he was advised to take up an independent study, and learn about something new. This investigation led him to Papua New Guinea.

Dan was attracted to what was then termed an "inhospitable" area. Simply put, an area where others did not want to go. The area needed to be investigated but living there was not an option. The government sequestered the area. The state's reason: cannibal-ism. Eventually, the sequester was lifted, and the area opened up for travel. It was 1969 and Dan left to study the region and its 800+ different languages and cultures.

Dan determined to conduct an in-depth language study. He compiled word lists to understand and see the connections between many of the languages in the country. He next focused his research on a small geographic region along the Strickland River in the Western Province of Papua New Guinea. Remote is an understatement.

It started raining very hard on December 8, 1969. At that point, he didn't know how significant this would be. It rained and rained, and it didn't stop until over 8 inches of rain fell. The rain caused so much flooding that only one path was left open for Dan to take. Dan heard a voice in his head to 'go north and cross the river.' God clearly directed Dan to the place where he was to go. God knew, but to Dan, one direction seemed as good as another.

The importance of going north soon became apparent. The different languages along the way had connective dialects. This universal connectivity enabled Dan to communicate easily with all the people groups along the river and was critical to the work he was being called to do. God plans our path long before we recognize the direction we are to go.

The next few years were productive and satisfying, although often physically and psychologically challenging. Mapping the multiple languages along the Strickland River allowed Dan and his team to begin translating the Bible for all the people along the river. This was his mission, his call: bringing God's life-giving message to the people of New Guinea in their heart language.

That epic rainfall that dictated Dan's original direction in December 1969 was the key. Going north, Dan traveled to the middle of the river where the dialect was such that tribes in the north and the south of the river could contextually understand. It was the language of the center—the language that would reach the most people. God directed Dan's mission and led him to the place of convergence. Dan witnessed the people of Papua New Guinea embrace the word of

God by connecting it to their culture.

Translating the Bible is not only translation but also contextualization. Finding words with the right meaning is call equivalency. It is critical for the reader, or listener, to understand both the words and their meaning. Years later, Dan went back to Papua New Guinea. He was blessed to see how the translation blessed the people and how the interpretation remained true to the original meaning. God's leading, his following, and a lot of hard work resulted in changing the everyday lives of the people and tribes along the Strickland River for generations.

When Dan shares his story, he often refers to himself and his family as "poor missionaries," a self-deprecating and completely tongue-in-cheek way of saying how fortunate he was to be able to have such an incredible impact. Dan connected with Future Funded Ministry nearly 25 years ago. He recognized the need to prepare for what was then called The Golden Years. He figuratively went North and discovered the connectivity between the funding of future ministry and God's plan for that future.

Over the course of a long and impactful teaching career, Dan has experienced the rewards of the work he started in Papua New Guinea. He also realized how a Future Funded Ministry would allow him to revisit past projects and to start new ones. Walking in faith and prepared for action is a great way to live. Lives continue to change as a result of Dan's willingness to go North. Now with adequate funding, he continues to respond by still saying, "send me." I recently met with Dan (now in his 80s), and he is still excited about his next trip back to Papua New Guinea.

8

Going from Black & White to Color HD

Pastor David Perkins remembers the confusion he felt trying to understand personal finance. It was not his calling, but he knew it was important. He has a vivid memory of sitting in an investment firm's office, trying to understand his options for funding his future. His church had a retirement plan but how it worked was not connecting. As they were talking about investments and saving for the future, none of the information was sinking in. It did not make sense to him because it was not aligned with his vision for the future. What he wanted was to save for a future of ministry. A lifetime of ministry. A lifetime of ministry built on a stable financial platform allowing him the freedom to follow God's call, wherever that might lead.

Never once did the investment representative speak of what he saw as David's vision. The representative talked about David's family and the freedom for him to have a self-absorbed retirement. Not David's priority at all. Their very secular approach to retirement planning didn't include encouraging David to pursue his deepest passion—reaching young people and helping them find Jesus. This is the one thing he plans on doing for the rest of his life. He wanted the retirement plan to be part of his ministry future. Not one designed to finance the end of his career.

David believes firmly that the Lord has called him to ministry for life, not just for a season or a moment. His life's calling is to share the word of God with every person willing to accept Jesus into their hearts and lives and beyond. To achieve his goals and continue his evangelical mission for the rest of his life, he knows that proper planning is the key to fulfilling that vision. It's important to his success. He has witnessed first-hand the power of God's most awesome love when young people accept Jesus. He sees how this new relationship with Jesus changes them for the better and forever. This is his calling. And he doesn't plan on stopping this ministry—ever.

The message of Future Funded Ministry spoke directly to David's needs. There are very few firms who understand, encourage, and support David's goals. One of them is Envoy Financial whose slogan of Trusted Advice Along The Way ties directly to David's needs. Connecting with a financial services ministry helped him understand the value and intricacies of the investment process. And, what is needed to make his future line up with his goals. Before Future Funded Ministry, investment planning seemed like a black and white TV to David. Future Funded Ministry sent everything into full-color HD.

Future Funded Ministry is enabling David to plan and follow his calling, knowing that he will be able to minister for the rest of his life. David will be able to spend his older years continuing the work and fulfilling that calling. The message of Future Funded Ministry spoke to David about his future not in the abstract but in concrete terms that made sense to him. If he wanted to continue to follow his calling, if he wanted to continue to minister into his retirement life stages, he had to plan now.

In David's eyes, there is no age limit for ministry. As he witnessed with his father, people want to stay engaged and continue to do the work they believe in, no matter their age. His goal is to continue ministering through his older years, and Future Funded Ministry is enabling him to prepare for this. The passion for ministry doesn't subside with age; it only gets stronger. David believes that Future Funded Ministry will allow him to keep doing the good work God has called him to, no matter his age.

David's passion for being a pastor starts with his family. They are a priority. Caring for them is high on the list of priorities. The Lord has a calling on the lives of each of his four children, and David wants to make sure they are empowered for a lifetime. Whatever their callings, he wants to provide the support they need. He suspects that those callings might have significant price tags attached, and he wants to be prepared. Future Funded Ministry is helping David be responsible and plan for his children's callings in life, as well as his own. As he continues to minister, his children will hear what God's plan is for them—and David wants to support that plan. Future Funded Ministry will be there to help.

David loves being God's representative. He embraces the power of God's word and how it impacts people—in particular, seeing young people become transformed when they bring Jesus into their lives. David is passionate about transformation. Through the ministry programs that he is a part of, David sees millions of people in multiple countries learn about Jesus. The result is changed lives—lots of them. That kind of high-impact ministry is what David is all about now and what he will be all about until the end of his days.

David sees Future Funded Ministry as his reassurance that he will be able to minister and pastor for the rest of his life. In later years, this will be his assurance that he will be able to continue spreading God's word and take any position at any ministry. Future Funded Ministry also puts David's mind at ease, knowing that he will be able to take care of his children and guide them along whatever path God has planned for them. For David, ministry is his life's calling, and he knows he will keep doing it as long as he can. Future Funded Ministry ensures David will be a minister until the end.

9

A Professional Perspective

Kim serves as Human Resources Manager of the First Baptist Church of Glenarden in Marlborough, Maryland. Her ministry began there in 2007. A longtime member of the FBC Glenarden congregation, Kim confesses that she feels blessed to work at her church so ably led by Pastor John Jenkins, Sr. She also serves the same role (HR Manager) for the Church's SHABACH! Ministries. SHABACH provides human services programs for children, youth, individuals, and families throughout Prince George's County, Maryland.

Kim Robinson is an HR professional. She worked for large corporations in the DC area before stepping into her ministry role at the church. Kim knows how hard it is to hire the right people and provide the right benefits for them. With over 1000 hires in her rear-view mirror, she looks out the front window with a wonderful, positive attitude. Her church is home to over 12,000 members and requires a large support staff. FBC Glenarden and SHABACH Ministries share over 300 paid and volunteer employees in order to keep operations for the church running smoothly! Kim is part of a great ministry team and is actively involved in the recruiting and hiring of almost all of those associates.

When she joined the staff in 2007, they were opening their worship center in Upper Marlborough, Maryland. This new building was in response to the growing size of the church. Their original church (which is now the business center where Kim works) is in Landover, Maryland and had a sanctuary with room for about 1,000 people per service. The new church offers space for up to 4,000 worshipers for each service, and they have four services on the weekend to provide flexibility for their congregation. This is a very big church, and she credits the growth to the leadership of Pastor John K. Jenkins, Sr. (Kim notes Pastor Jenkins is an incredibly humble man who would never take credit for what this church has become).

Kim has personally witnessed the church grow from around 1,000 members to what it is today and notes that it's because the pastor delivers "a real, relevant word that will impact your life" every week.

Pastor Jenkins is another Future Funded Ministry Champion.

Kim inherited the idea of Future Funded Ministry as part of the Envoy Financial retirement plan. Pastor Jenkins and the original finance team put this plan in place a few years before her employment. She likes to tell everyone who asks that their Future Funded Ministry plan contributes to all full-time employees whether they choose to participate or not.

Kim was a new staff member when she inherited the plan and says that she didn't even know that there were Christians who created retirement plans that were purposefully faith-based. She admits that she wasn't sure a Christian-driven plan was needed but came quickly to understand the difference, realizing that you do need professionals who understand ministry to serve every Christian worker at the church.

"People don't retire from ministry," Kim says, "They

will do ministry until the day they die, and how are they going to do that without finances?" She affirms Envoy because they understand the church and understand how nonprofits work. This understanding enables them to be able to serve their most ardent believers. Envoy understands the unique needs of ministers and speaks the language of the plan participants. Envoy also recognizes the importance of administering the unique housing allowance distributions available to ministers and pastors.

First Baptist Church of Glenarden truly stands for a higher purpose and spiritual meaning. Kim loves her church and feels like it is a major blessing and a privilege to work there. This is a church where her pastor and first lady raised six children, and they've allowed Kim an opportunity to both raise her family and give back to the kingdom of God, and that's what she calls a privilege. She has watched the church grow and has seen the pastor's vision surpass his wildest expectations. She expresses that she is privileged to see what God does every day and see how His word changes the lives of all kinds of people in a significant way.

Kim is a person of faith, learning at a young age from her community church choir experience that there was so much more to being a Christian than she realized. In fact, as a teenager, she first came to sing at First Baptist Church of Glenarden and was so impressed that she felt like she needed to visit on a Sunday. Not too many years later she became a member.

The thing that brings Kim the most joy at this stage in her life is watching her staff grow and seeing them develop both spiritually and professionally. She says that is why Future Funded Ministry is so important. Not only does it make retirement palatable, but it also makes planning for years of future ministry easy to understand and worth the investment.

Kim has been more serious about retirement planning than most of her peers. She started contributing to a 401K and other plans since she was 22 years old, routinely increasing contribution as her pay increased. She admits that it wasn't until her experience with Envoy Financial that she understood why. Envoy's message has put it into perspective that one day her paycheck is going to end, and if she wants to continue her ministry (and she does) she will only be able to afford it if she saves for it today. Kim would like to go on a mission trip someday and would love to volunteer for the Empowerment Center at SHABACH!

Ministries. That is, of course, when she can carve the time to do so, and that means in retirement.

All Christians are called to ministry for a lifetime, according to Kim. She even calls herself the Minister of HR and considers it her duty to put the right retirement plan in place for her church. She knows in her heart that Future Funded Ministry is just that—the right plan. She has thoroughly enjoyed her relationship with the people of Envoy Financial, explaining that Envoy believes and loves what it does and is passionate about it.

For Kim, she knows that it's her responsibility to fund her future in ministry. "God does not retire you; you still have a responsibility to spread the Gospel, change lives, and put a plan together to take care of your family, and yes, to embrace that time of life when you are slowing down a bit." That is the heart of Future Funded Ministry—powerful, indeed.

A.W. Tozer in his classic book, "The Pursuit of God" says it this way:

"The moment we make up our minds that we are going on with the determination to exalt God over

all, we step out of the world's parade. We shall find ourselves out of adjustment to the ways of the world, and increasingly so as we make progress in the holy way. We shall acquire a new viewpoint; a new and different way to think will be formed within us; a new power will begin to surprise us by its upsurgings and its outgoings."

Yes, powerful indeed!

So why have we shared what it means to be a committed Christian in ministry, and why have we reiterated what it means to be called for a lifetime by God? Why did we take you through the painful experiences that were the sad reality of poor planning—our reality checks? And why did we show you what it means to be wonderful and encouraging role models? It is to help you experience the lives of every day ministers that believe so firmly in what I write about and Envoy encourages. These are a sampling of the thousands we are so proud to call Future Funded Ministry Champions.

10

The DNA of Meaning Drives Our Future

It comes down to this: when we have an emotional connection to inspiring people, it helps us remember the pivotal moments, the good and bad decisions, and the powerful memories of our own lives. These are the kind of relationships, connections, and profound experiences that shape our individual and collective lives. This starts to describe the DNA of meaning and is the raw material that creates a lifetime filled with purpose. Where does the energy come from to move us forward, in God's direction? The energy to get out of bed, off the chair, and into the next stage of life?

Regardless of where we are in those final three stages of life, regardless of our physical status, or our cognitive acuity, we are called to "pick up our bed and walk."

We are all different. We have different life experiences, perceptions, and even DNA to both prepare us for and take us down different life paths. It is therefore reasonable for those very experiences and our unique DNA to propel us into different futures.

Think about it, a basic definition of DNA is:

1. The fundamental and distinctive characteristics or qualities of someone or something, especially when understood as unchangeable;

2. The biological instructions that make each person unique.

The circumstances in which meaningful, memorable, and impactful experiences are created bring joy and sorrow, pain and pleasure, and guidance and chaos to our lives. The DNA of meaning provides context. Think of it this way: a unique set of emotions prompts action, and our minds prompt process. Our future actions must have enough meaning and emotional connection for them to become a priority. In order for any future action to become a priority, it must have meaning and emotional connection. That is The DNA of meaning for us: life with purpose.

What joy it is to understand that living is about serving God and achieving meaningful results in our lives while impacting others for good. Because we are likely to live a long time, we want to reflect in our actions the events that bring meaning for the entirety of our days. Getting you to an understanding of your life's purpose (His plan for you) is one of the most important reasons I wrote this book. Meaning—His purpose—is something that will continue to drive you and is something that you can live out for your entire life. You do have to prepare. You do have to fund your future service and to have a meaningful life filled with purpose until the very end.

That is the power of Future Funded Ministry. A call to a lifetime of action, to the very end.

So we will end this first eBook with this thought directly from my blog post on the DNA of meaning:

How much and what kind of meaning is sufficient to

prompt action? We believe the decisions we make and the actions we take are inextricably intertwined with the meaning and purpose we give to them. At a subconscious level, we understand the need to take action and plan for retirement. Our actions, however, speak louder than out words. The annual Faith-Based Retirement Plan Survey results suggest that most don't take much action. Just like planning for retirement, the standard is nothing. We each need to examine our motives and action plans.

While so many don't take action, you can be the exception. As a Future Funded Ministry champion in the making, your life can change. A changed life will impact others. You can make a difference—a new dream can replace the doldrums of indifference.

By connecting an action plan to event triggers filled with memory means you can embark on a journey of discovery and preparation. These are the very first steps to helping you put a Future Funded Ministry Plan in place allowing greater freedom to follow God's call on your life—to the very end.

You also, like living stones, are being built into a spiritual house, to be a holy leader, offering spiritual works acceptable to God through Jesus Christ.

1 Peter 2:5.

Therefore we conclude—you are the personal work of His hands, being shaped by Him, and destined for the purpose of good works prepared by God for you to complete.

This is the life journey that is Future Funded Ministry. So here is the challenge: are you going to fulfill that call to live life with meaning? Are you going to bring your experiences to life-changing ministry? The insights, suggestions, and encouragement I've shared will make a difference if you remain open to God's leading, the wisdom from the Bible, and the encouragement of the thousands of others who are on this journey too.

Look for the next book in the series, a more in-depth explanation, and encouraging word about Moving Forward: How to Put Your Future Funded Ministry Into Motion.

About Bruce Bruinsma

Bruce is the Founder of Envoy Financial and the Live with Meaning Foundation, which inspire and empower people for a lifetime of ministry. In addition, he is the co-creator of several businesses that financially support ministries and communities in the United States, Europe, and Asia.

Bruce holds an MBA from the University of California, Berkeley and has more than 40 years of professional experience in retirement planning and finance. He is the authors of three books, consults with Christian ministries worldwide, and is a sought-after presenter. Currently, he lives in Colorado with his wife Judy.

For more information, go to BruceBruinsma.com

The Retirement Reformation

Our calling to love and serve others doesn't end at retirement. In fact, retirement could be the season of your life where you have the greatest impact for God's Kingdom. You have unique passions, abilities, and experiences that God wants to use in ALL seasons and stages of your life.

Discover your calling. Maximize your life. Change your world. Join the Retirement Reformation at RetirementReformation.org.

28739684R00059

Made in the USA
Lexington, KY
20 January 2019